Riverdale School
8901 - 101 Avenue
Edmonton, Alberta
T5H 0B1

It's Spring

Sharon Callen

spring

summer

fall

The Seasons

There are four seasons in a year. They are spring, summer, fall, and winter.

winter

Is it spring where you are today?

Spring Weather Words

These words help us to describe spring weather.

rainy

sunny

cloudy

breezy

windy

warm

mild

cool

Spring Weather Watchers

We watch the weather every day. Weather is made up of different things such as clouds, sunshine, wind, and temperature.

What is the weather like where you are today?

OUR CLASS WEATHER CHART

wetter

better

calm   breezy   windy

Temperature

hot
warm
mild
cool
cold
freezing

TODAY is

WARM

and

CLOUDY

5

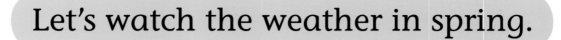

Let's watch the weather in spring.

Monday, April 7

Today it is rainy.
It is breezy and cool.

OUR CLASS WEATHER CHART

calm | **breezy** | windy

Temperature
- hot
- warm
- mild
- cool
- cold
- freezing

TODAY
is
COOL
and
RAINY

Tuesday, April 8

Today it is cloudy.
It is windy and cool.

OUR CLASS WEATHER CHART

calm   breezy   windy

Temperature
hot
warm
mild
cool
cold
freezing

TODAY
is
COOL
and
CLOUDY

Wednesday, April 9

Today it is sunny.
It is windy and warm.

10

OUR CLASS WEATHER CHART

WEDNESDAY APRIL 9

calm   breezy   windy

Temperature

hot
warm
mild
cool
cold
freezing

TODAY
is
WARM
and
SUNNY

Thursday, April 10

Today it is sunny.
It is calm and mild.

OUR CLASS WEATHER CHART

wetter

better

calm   breezy   windy

Temperature

hot
warm
mild
cool
cold
freezing

TODAY
is

MILD

and

SUNNY

Friday, April 11

Today it is cloudy.
It is windy and warm.

OUR CLASS WEATHER CHART

wetter → better

calm　　breezy　　**windy**

Temperature

- hot
- **warm**
- mild
- cool
- cold
- freezing

TODAY
is
WARM
and
CLOUDY

Are you a
spring weather
watcher?

16